Hymns & Spirituals

HAS1

Wise Publications
London/New York/Paris/Sydney/Copenhagen/Madrid

Exclusive Distributors:
Music Sales Limited
8/9 Frith Street, London W1V 5TZ, England.
Music Sales Pty Limited
120 Rothschild Avenue, Rosebery, NSW 2018, Australia.
Music Sales Corporation
257 Park Avenue South, New York, NY10010, United States of America.

This book © Copyright 1994 by Wise Publications
Order No. AM91983
ISBN 0-7119-4099-1

Cover design by Hutton & Partners
Music arranged by Stephen Duro
Music processed by Allegro Reproductions

Cover photograph courtesy of
Ace Photo Agency

Music Sales' complete catalogue describes thousands of titles and is available in full colour sections by subject,
direct from Music Sales Limited. Please state your areas of interest and send a cheque/postal order for £1.50 for
postage to: Music Sales Limited, Newmarket Road, Bury St. Edmunds, Suffolk IP33 3YB.

All Things Bright And Beautiful

Words by C. F. Alexander. Music by W. H. Monk

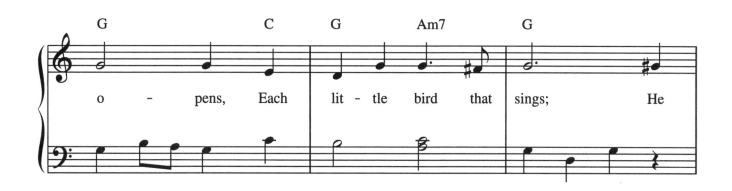

o - pens, Each lit - tle bird that sings; He

D.S. al Fine

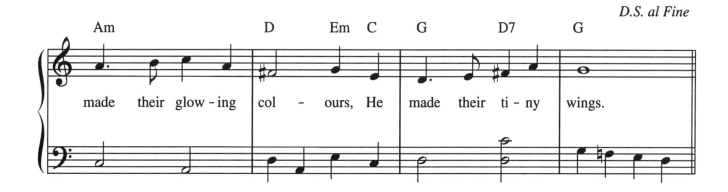

made their glow - ing col - ours, He made their ti - ny wings.

3. The purple headed mountain,
   The river running by;
   The sunset and the morning
   That brightens up the sky:
   All things bright *etc.*

4. The cold wind in the winter,
   The pleasant summer sun,
   The ripe fruits in the garden,
   He made them ev'ry one:
   All things bright *etc.*

5. The tall trees in the greenwood,
   The meadows where we play,
   The rushes by the water
   We gather ev'ry day:
   All things bright *etc.*

6. He gave us eyes to see them,
   And lips that we might tell
   How great is God Almighty,
   Who has made all things well:
   All things bright *etc.*

Blow Your Trumpet, Gabriel

Traditional

Deep River

Traditional

Slow and expressive

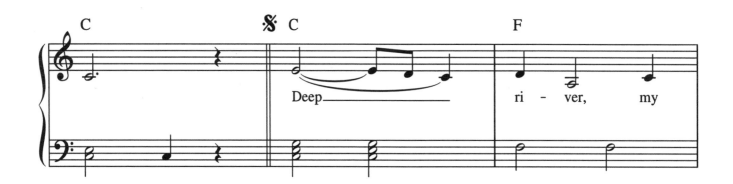

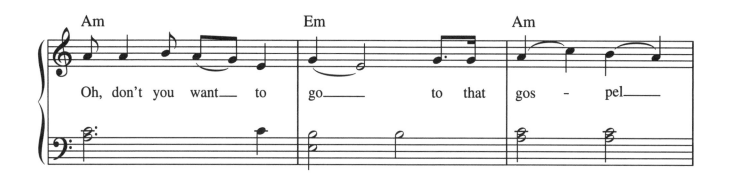

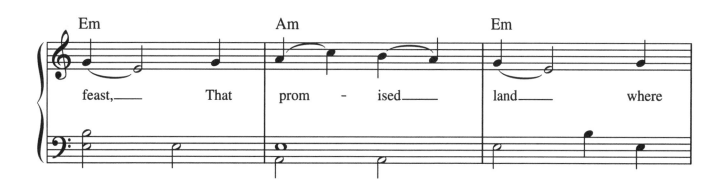

D.S. al Fine

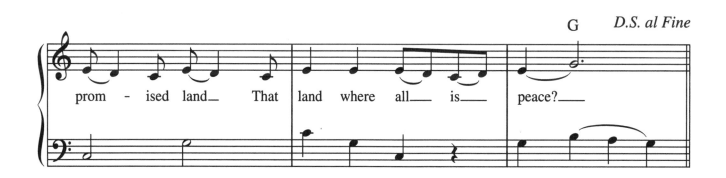

Eternal Father, Strong To Save

Words by W. Whiting. Music by J. B. Dykes

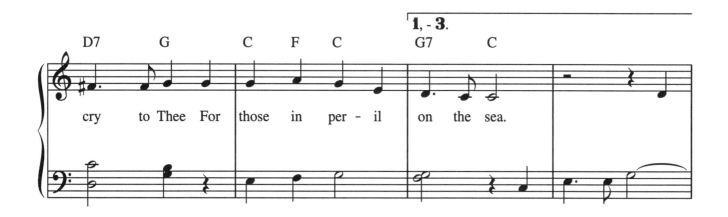

cry   to Thee For those in per - il   on   the   sea.

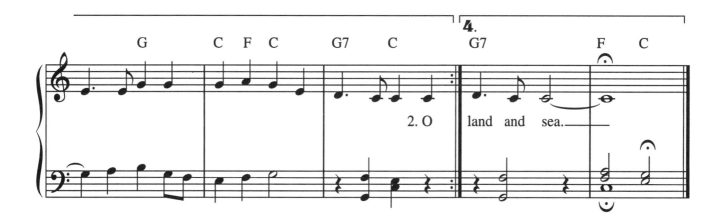

2. O   land   and sea.

2. O Saviour whose almighty word
   The winds and waves submissive heard,
   Who walkedst on the foaming deep
   And calm amid its rage did sleep:
   O hear us when we cry to Thee
   For those in peril on the sea.

3. O sacred Spirit, who didst brood
   Upon the waters dark and rude,
   And bid their angry tumult cease,
   And give, for wild confusion, peace:
   O hear us when we cry to Thee
   For those in peril on the sea.

4. O Trinity of love and power,
   Our brethren shield in danger's hour:
   From rock and tempest, fire and foe,
   Protect them wheresoe'er they go;
   And ever let there rise to Thee
   Glad hymns of praise from land and sea.

Git On Board, Little Children

Traditional

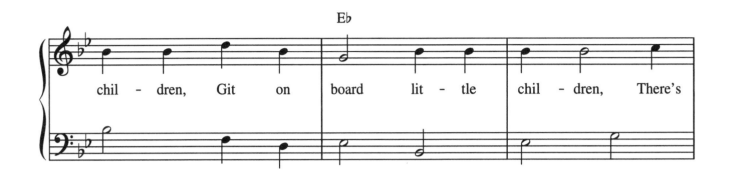

chil - dren, Git on board lit - tle chil - dren, There's

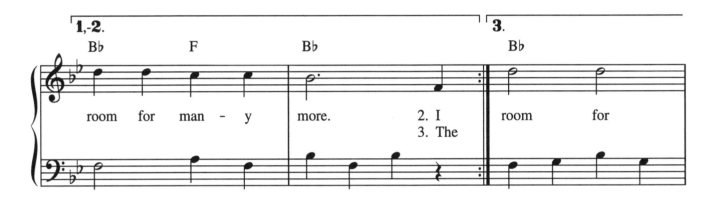

room for man - y more. 2. I 3. The room for

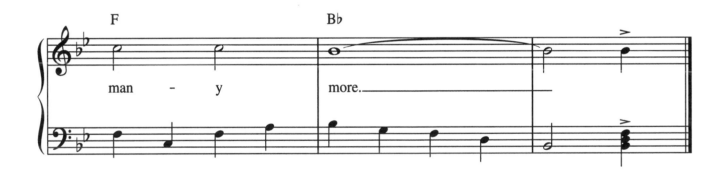

man - y more.

2. I heard the train's a-comin',
   She's comin' 'round the curve,
   She's loosen'd all her steam and brakes,
   And strainin' ev'ry nerve.
      Chorus: Git on board, ... *etc.*

3. The fare is cheap an' all can go,
   The rich and poor are there,
   No second class aboard this train,
   No diff'rence in the fare.
      Chorus: Git on board, ... *etc.*

Go Down, Moses

Traditional

Slowly

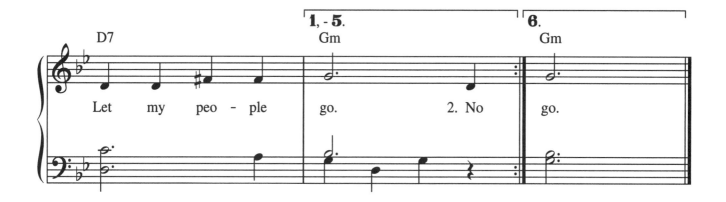

2. No more shall they in bondage toil,
   Let my people go.
   Let them come out with Egypt's spoil,
   Let my people go.
       Chorus: Go down, Moses ..... *etc.*

3. When Israel out of Egypt came,
   Let my people go.
   And left the proud offensive land,
   Let my people go.
       Chorus: Go down, Moses ..... *etc.*

4. 'Twas good old Moses and Aaron, too,
   Let my people go.
   'Twas they that led the armies through,
   Let my people go.
       Chorus: Go down, Moses ..... *etc.*

5. O come along, Moses, you'll not get lost,
   Let my people go.
   Stretch out your rod and come across,
   Let my people go.
       Chorus: Go down, Moses ..... *etc.*

6. Pharaoh said he'd go across,
   Let my people go.
   But Pharaoh and his host were lost,
   Let my people go.
       Chorus: Go down, Moses ..... *etc.*

Go Tell It On The Mountains

Traditional

With movement

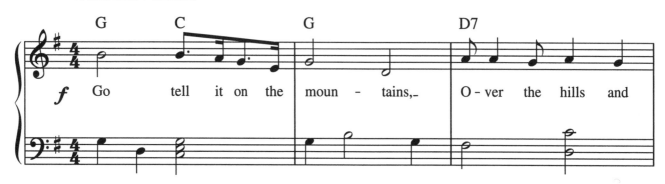

Go tell it on the moun - tains,_ O - ver the hills and

ev - 'ry - where, Go tell it on the moun - tains, Our

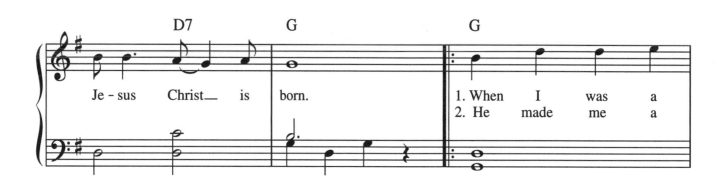

Je - sus Christ__ is born.

1. When I was a
2. He made me a

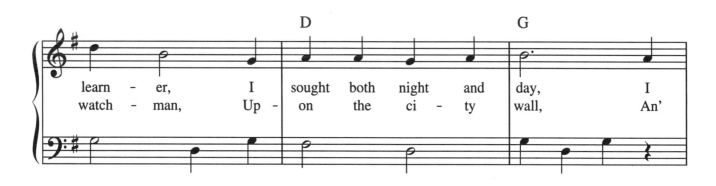

learn - er, I sought both night and day, I
watch - man, Up - on the ci - ty wall, An'

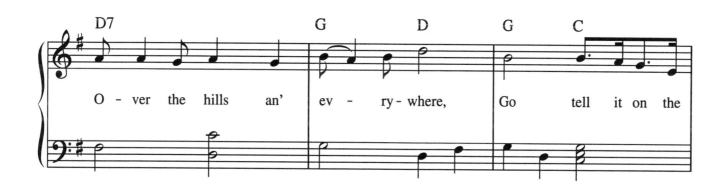

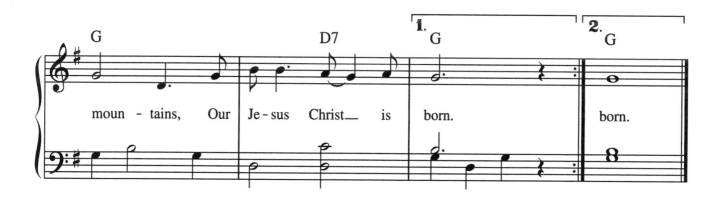

He Who Would Valiant Be

Words by John Bunyan to the traditional tune "Monks Gate"

2. Who so beset him round
   With dismal stories,
   Do but themselves confound:
   His strength the more is.
   No foes shall stay his might,
   Though he with giants fight
   He will make good his right
   To be a Pilgrim.

3. Since, Lord, Thou dost defend
   Us with Thy Spirit,
   We know we at the end
   Shall life inherit.
   Then fancies flee away,
   I'll fear not what men say,
   I'll labour night and day
   To be a Pilgrim.

Joshua Fight The Battle Of Jericho

Traditional

soun',   Josh - ua   com - man - ded   the   chil - dren   to   shout,   An' the

walls   come   tum - blin'   down!   Josh - ua   fight   the   bat - tle   of___

Je - ri - cho,___   Je - ri - cho,___   Je - ri - cho.___

Josh - ua   fight   the   bat - tle   of___   Je - ri - cho,_   An' the   walls   come   tum - blin'

down.   walls   come   tum - blin'   down.___

Little David, Play On Your Harp

Traditional

All People That On Earth Do Dwell

Words by W. Kethe to the tune "Old 100th"

With grandeur

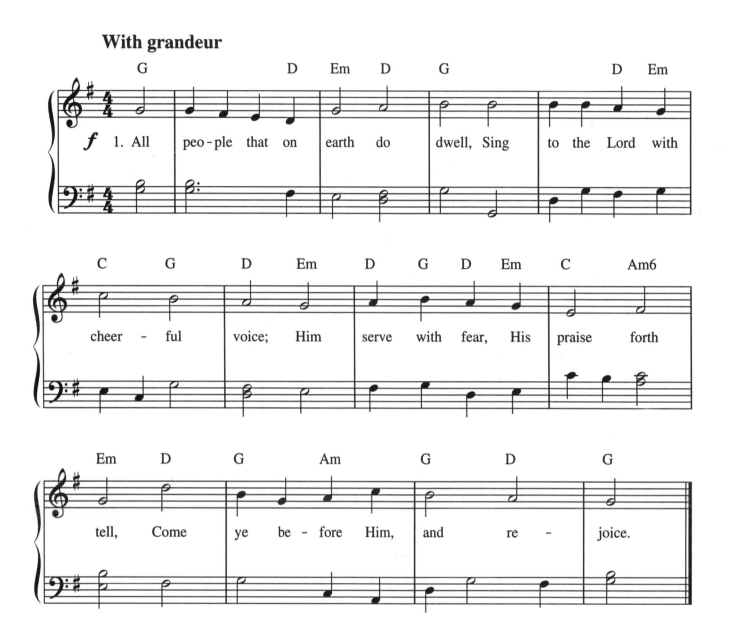

2. The Lord, ye know, is God indeed;
   Without our aid He did us make;
   We are His folk, He doth us feed,
   And for His sheep He doth us take.

3. O enter then His gates with praise,
   Approach with joy His courts unto:
   Praise, laud and bless His name always,
   For it is seemly so to do.

4. For why? the Lord our God is Good;
   His mercy is for ever sure:
   His truth at all times firmly stood,
   And shall from age to age endure.

5. To Father, Son, and Holy Ghost,
   The God whom heaven and earth adore,
   From men and from the angel-host
   Be praise and glory evermore.

Nobody Knows The Trouble I See

Traditional

Moderately with expression

No - bo - dy knows the trou - ble I see, No - bo - dy knows but

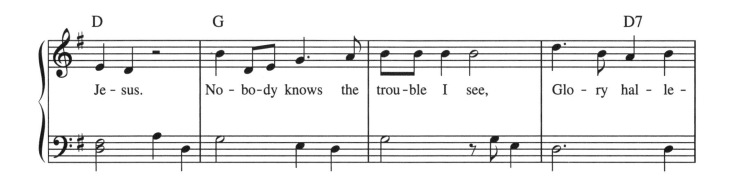

Je - sus. No - bo - dy knows the trou - ble I see, Glo - ry hal - le -

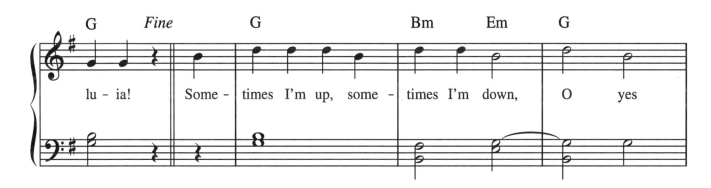

lu - ia! Some - times I'm up, some - times I'm down, O yes

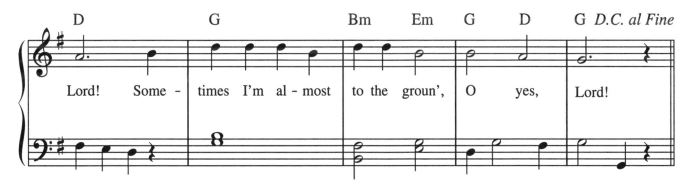

Lord! Some - times I'm al - most to the groun', O yes, Lord!

Mine Eyes Have Seen The Glory

Words by J. W. Howe. Melody attributed to W. Steffe

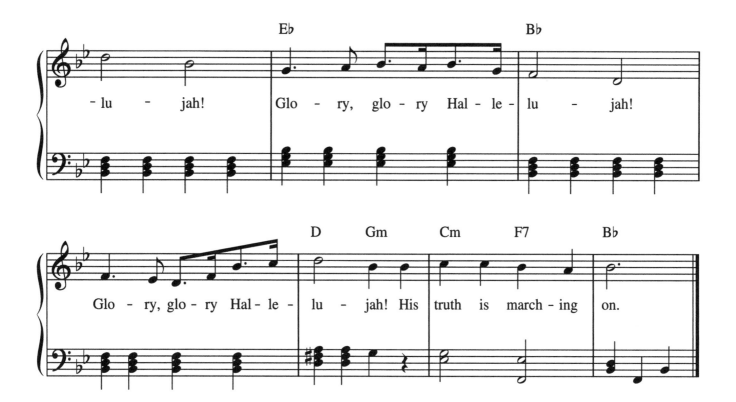

2. I've seen Him in the watch-fires of a hundred circling camps,
   They have builded Him an altar in the evening dews and damps;
   I have read His righteous sentence by the dim and flaring lamps,
   His day is marching on.
   Glory, glory, Hallelujah! *etc.*

3. I have read a fiery gospel writ in burnished rows of steel,
   "As ye deal with My contemner, so with you My grace shall deal."
   Let the hero born of woman crush the serpent with His heel,
   Since God is marching on.
   Glory, glory, Hallelujah! *etc.*

4. He hath sounded forth the trumpet that shall never call retreat;
   He is sifting out the hearts of men before His judgement seat;
   O, be swift, my soul, to answer Him: be jubilant, my feet!
   Our God is marching on.
   Glory, glory, Hallelujah! *etc.*

5. In the beauty of the lilies Christ was born, across the sea,
   With a glory in His bosom that transfigures you and me;
   As He died to make men holy, let us live to make men free,
   While God is marching on.
   Glory, glory, Hallelujah! *etc.*

Standin' In The Need Of Pray'r

Traditional

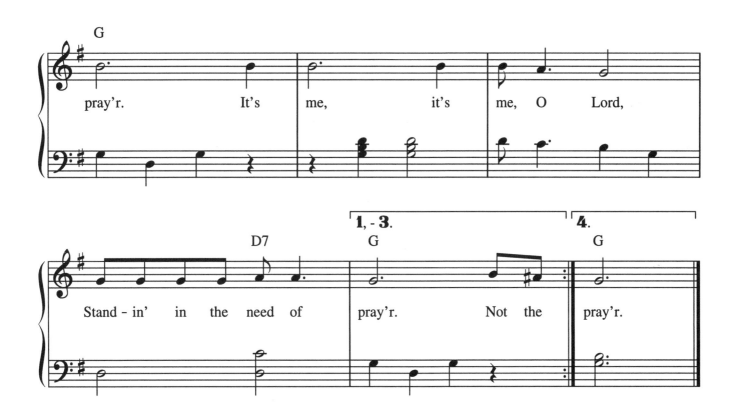

2. Not the preacher, nor the deacon, but it's me, O Lord,
   Standin' in the need of pray'r.
      Chorus: It's me, ... *etc.*

3. Not my father, nor my mother, but it's me, O Lord,
   Standin' in the need of pray'r.
      Chorus: It's me, ... *etc.*

4. Not the stranger, nor my neighbour, but it's me, O Lord,
   Standin' in the need of pray'r.
      Chorus: It's me, ... *etc.*

Stand Up, Stand Up For Jesus

Words by G. Duffield. Music by G. J. Webb

Moderately

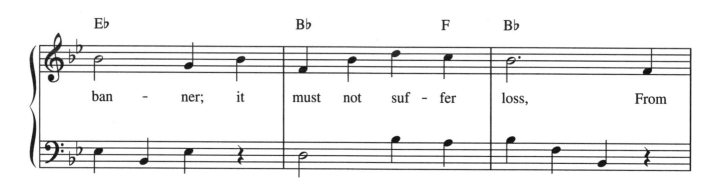

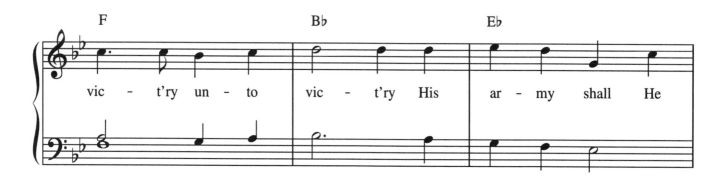

2. Stand up, stand up for Jesus,
   The trumpet call obey;
   Forth to the mighty conflict
   In this His glorious day.
   Ye that are men now serve Him
   Against the unnumbered foes;
   Your courage rise with danger,
   And strength to strength oppose.

3. Stand up, stand up for Jesus,
   Stand in His strength alone;
   The arm of flesh will fail you,
   Ye dare not trust your own.
   Put on the gospel armour,
   Each piece put on with prayer;
   Where duty calls or danger,
   Be never wanting there.

4. Stand up, stand up for Jesus,
   Each soldier to his post;
   Close up the broken column
   And shout through all the host.
   Make good the loss so heavy
   In those that still remain;
   And prove to all around you
   That death itself is gain.

5. Stand up, stand up for Jesus,
   The strife will not be long;
   This day the noise of battle,
   The next the victor's song.
   To him that overcometh
   A crown of life shall be:
   He with the King of Glory
   Shall reign eternally.

Rock Of Ages

Words by A. M. Toplady. Music by R. Redhead

3. Nothing in my hand I bring,
   Simply to Thy Cross I cling;
   Naked, come to Thee for dress:
   Helpless, look to Thee for grace;
   Foul, I to the fountain fly;
   Wash me, Saviour, or I die.

4. While I draw this fleeting breath,
   When mine eyes shall close in death,
   When I soar through tracts unknown,
   See Thee on Thy judgement throne,
   Rock of ages, cleft for me,
   Let me hide myself in Thee.

Steal Away To Jesus

Traditional

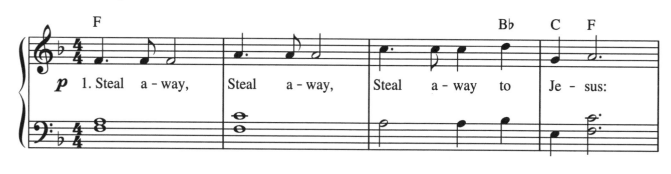

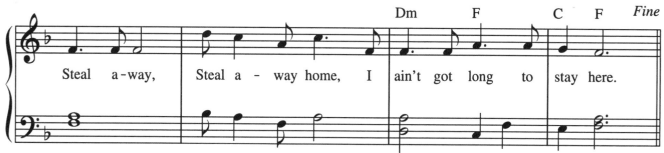

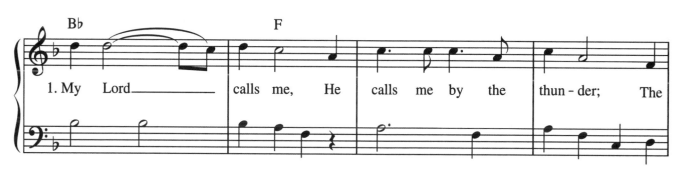

2. Green trees are bending,
   Poor sinners stand trembling,
   The trumpet sounds within my soul
   I ain't got long to stay here.
      Chorus: Steal away ..... *etc.*

3. My Lord calls me,
   He calls me by the lightning.
   The trumpet sounds within my soul
   I ain't got long to stay here.
      Chorus: Steal away ..... *etc.*

Swing Low, Sweet Chariot

Traditional

2. If you get there before I do,
    Coming for to carry me home,
    Tell all my friends I'm coming too,
    Coming for to carry me home.
        Chorus: Swing low, ... etc.

3. The brightest day that I ever saw,
    Coming for to carry me home,
    When Jesus washed my sins away,
    Coming for to carry me home.
        Chorus: Swing low, ... etc.

4. I'm sometimes up and sometimes down,
    Coming for to carry me home,
    But still my soul feels heavenly bound,
    Coming for to carry me home.
        Chorus: Swing low ..... etc.

Tell Me The Old, Old Story

Words by K. Hankey. Music by W. H. Doane

3. Tell me the story softly,
   With earnest tones and grave;
   Remember, I'm the sinner
   Whom Jesus came to save.
   Tell me the story always,
   If you would really be,
   In any time of trouble
   A comforter to me.
   Tell me the old, old story *etc.*

4. Tell me the same old story,
   When you have cause to fear,
   That this world's empty glory
   Is costing me too dear:
   Yes, and when that world's glory
   Is dawning on my soul,
   Tell me the old, old story:
   "Christ Jesus makes thee whole."
   Tell me the old, old story *etc.*

The Church's One Foundation

Words by S. J. Stone. Music by S. S. Wesley

be His ho - ly bride, With His own blood He

bought her, And for her life He died. 2. E - Thee.

2. Elect from ev'ry nation,
    Yet one o'er all the earth;
    Her charter of salvation
    One Lord, one faith, one birth;
    One holy name she blesses,
    Partakes one holy food,
    And to one hope she presses
    With ev'ry grace endued.

4. 'Mid toil and tribulation,
    And tumult of her war,
    She waits the consummation
    Of peace for evermore;
    Till with the vision glorious
    Her longing eyes are blest,
    And the great Church victorious
    Shall be the Church at rest.

3. Though with a scornful wonder
    Men see her sore oppressed,
    By schisms rent asunder,
    By heresies distressed,
    Yet saints their watch are keeping,
    Their cry goes up, "How long?"
    And soon the night of weeping
    Shall be the morn of song.

5. Yet she on earth hath union
    With God the Three in One
    And mystic sweet communion
    With those whose rest is won:
    O happy ones and holy!
    Lord give us grace that we
    Like them, the meek and lowly,
    On high may dwell with Thee.

We Plough The Fields And Scatter

Words by M. Claudius. Music by A. P. Schulz

2. He only is the maker
   Of all things near and far,
   He paints the wayside flower,
   He lights the evening star.
   The winds and waves obey Him,
   By Him the birds are fed;
   Much more to us, His children,
   He gives our daily bread.
   All good gifts *etc.*

3. We thank Thee then, O Father,
   For all things bright and good;
   The seed-time and the harvest,
   Our life, our health, our food.
   No gifts have we to offer
   For all Thy love imparts,
   But that which Thou desirest,
   Our humble, thankful hearts.
   All good gifts *etc.*

Were You There?

Traditional

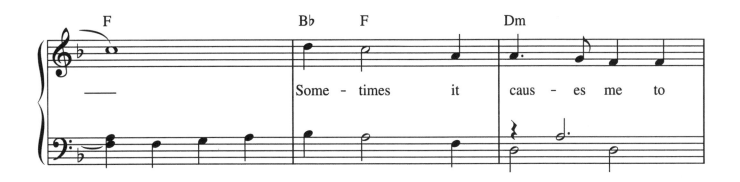

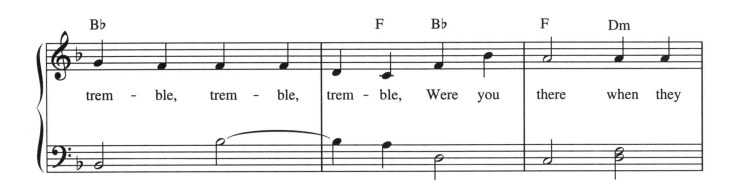

2. Were you there when they laid Him in the tomb?
   Were you there when they laid Him in the tomb?
   Oh, sometimes it causes me to tremble, tremble, tremble;
   Were you there when they laid Him in the tomb?

The Lord's My Shepherd

Words from the Scottish Psalter (1650). Music by J. S. Irvine

Moderately

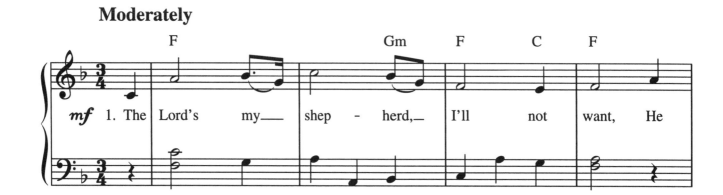

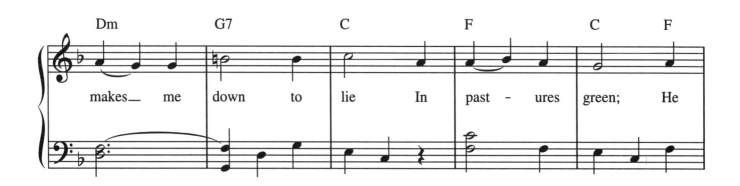

2. My soul He doth restore again,
   And me to walk doth make
   Within the paths of righteousness,
   E'en for His own name's sake.

3. Yea, though I walk in death's dark vale,
   Yet will I fear no ill;
   For Thou art with me, and Thy rod
   And staff me comfort still.

4. My table Thou has furnished
   In presence of my foes;
   My head Thou dost with oil anoint,
   And my cup overflows.

5. Goodness and mercy all my life
   Shall surely follow me;
   And in God's house for evermore
   My dwelling-place shall be.

When I Survey The Wondrous Cross

Words by I. Watts & Melody adapted by E. Miller

Slow

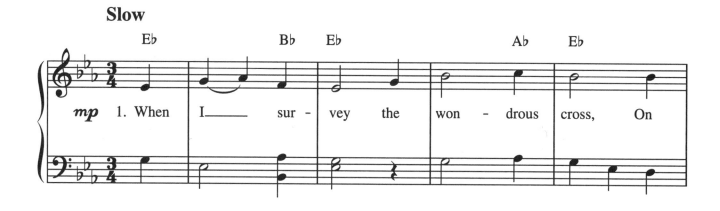

When I___ sur - vey the won - drous cross, On

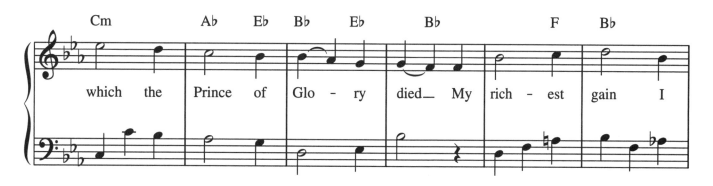

which the Prince of Glo - ry died__ My rich - est gain I

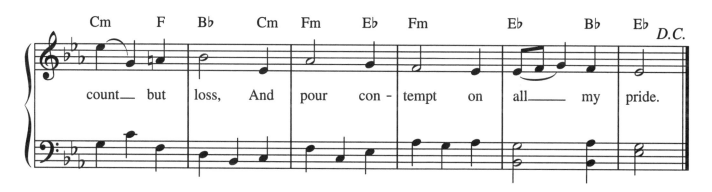

count__ but loss, And pour con - tempt on all___ my pride.

2. Forbid it Lord, that I should boast
Save in the death of Christ my God
All the vain things that charm me most,
I sacrifice them to His blood.

3. See from His head, His hands, His feet,
Sorrow and love flow mingled down;
Did e'er such love and sorrow meet,
Or thorns compose so rich a Crown?

4. His dying crimson, like a robe,
Spreads o'er His body on the Tree;
Then am I dead to all the globe,
And all the globe is dead to me.

5. Were the whole realm of nature mine,
That were a present far too small;
Love so amazing, so divine,
Demands my soul, my life, my all.

Each volume is specially arranged by Stephen Duro in extra-easy keys, so that the music fits comfortably to your hands, and includes lyrics (where appropriate) and chord symbols.

Collect the full series...

Abba *Order No. AM91038*
Bach *Order No. AM91041*
Ballads *Order No. AM89944*
Beethoven *Order No. AM91042*
Blues *Order No. AM91507*
Children's Songs *Order No. AM89953*
Richard Clayderman *Order No. AM91501*
Classics *Order No. AM89927*

Simply, the easiest books of popular music for piano ever!

Christmas *Order No. AM91509*
Folk Songs *Order No. AM91366*
Handel *Order No. AM91299*
Love Themes *Order No. AM91508*
Marches *Order No. AM91365*
Mozart *Order No. AM91043*
Operatic Arias *Order No. AM91312*
Pops *Order No. AM89939*
Rock 'n' Roll *Order No. AM91040*
Show Tunes *Order No. AM91039*
Symphonic Themes *Order No. AM91313*
Hits of the 50s *Order No. AM91502*
Hits of the 60s *Order No. AM91503*
Hits of the 70s *Order No. AM91504*
Hits of the 80s *Order No. AM91505*
The Beatles *Order No. AM89912*
The Beatles 2 *Order No. NO90571*
The Carpenters *Order No. AM91500*
TV Themes *Order No. AM89968*
Viennese Waltzes *Order No. AM91314*

Available from all good music shops

In case of difficulty, please contact:
Music Sales Limited
Newmarket Road,
Bury St. Edmunds,
Suffolk IP33 3YB, England
Telephone: 0284 702600
Fax: 0284 768301